Filling the Well

Elizabeth Durden

Thanks and Acknowledgements

Thank you Lord for forgiving me after 35 years of not knowing you, and forgiving me for allowing the norms of a fallen world to be my norms. Thank you for Your love, Your patience, Your grace, Your light, and Your forgiveness. I pray that all who read this are able to see Your light shining through me. Allow this book to be a lighthouse that all can see the way and the path to You.

My husband and my daughters are the most amazing people I could ever know. The love and devotion I have for them is everlasting. I thank them so much for giving me time and patience when I am not always the best I can be.

I thank my church family at Mount Vernon Baptist Church, my Team Mind over Matter family, and Pastor Steven Furtick for one small sentence he spoke that allowed God to show me this through the Pastors words.

INTRODUCTION

When I first heard God's calling for me to write a book, so many things ran through my mind.

What would I write about? Not knowing Him for 35 years? How to get out of debt? Finding your calling? Telling the story of a female in the Army? Being raped? Not feeling worthy? Having an eating disorder? Cutting? Being a lost teenager? Raising kids? Divorce? Remarriage? Trust issues? Knowing your fear is also your calling?

>Yes, this is all me. This is just some of MY story. There is so much more of me too.

We are all SO uniquely qualified to share our own story and our own testimony. We have such a diverse collection of issues and events, good and bad that make up who we are. What good does it do to hide it? It can eat you up inside if you let it. It can also free you if you let it. If me sharing this can help one person, that makes it worth it in Gods eyes. Which means it's worth it.

This book came about one day in the shower as I was praying to and talking with God. It all came at once. I had so much I wanted to get out before I forgot. Truthfully, this now is being typed into my phone right after that very shower.

I had started to talk text these words into my phone, to get it all out as quick as I could and I realized I can't even say some of these things out loud! We are all truly a work in progress, and no matter how hard we try, we always have room to grow. We are never done being better.

I have been told many times since I was a teenager that I should write a book. I have thought about it many times. But today, as I write this, God told me, and I am listening.

So as I wrap up this introduction, I tell you this: when God tells you to do something, do it.

Do not doubt God, doubt the doubt.

CHAPTER 1

What is "The Well"?

So, I know that you are asking, what well is this that I am speaking of? Well, let me tell you!

I can, like many of you, be told something a million times and not have it mean anything. But one person can say it in a certain way that allows me visualize it, and then it all falls into place. It all makes sense. Those things that people try and get you to understand all comes together like a light switch being flicked on.

Pastor Steven Furtick did a live video on Facebook not long ago, (as of the writing of this book) answering questions and <u>one statement</u> he made led to the light bulb moment God gave me to write this book.

He said something along the lines as, *if your well is empty you have nothing to give anyone*. As a health and fitness mentor and coach I share with people all the time that you have to take care of yourself first, to be able to take care of others, but this statement took it to a whole new level for me.

I have to be able to fill MY well first, before anyone else can take water from me. It hit me like a punch to the stomach. Nothing made sense like this visualization did. Join me for a minute here, and picture a well, where people from all over come to get water. They use the pulley system to put move the rope to lower the bucket into the water. You can picture that can't you? Picture that well is you.

Are you still with me? What if those people trek the entire way, only to find out that there is no water? Those people coming to you aren't getting anything. They aren't getting what they came for, what you promised to be from afar, what you portray yourself to be. They know you and see you in the distance, they know they can make the journey to you and you will satisfy their thirst.

But you can't do that if you are empty can you? Can you give your husband and children the attention and love they deserve if you don't give yourself love and attention? You may be able to fake it for a bit. But once they reach you from the distance and put that bucket all the way down to the bottom, they realize you are empty and have nothing to give. They are excited and built up with anticipation of the promise that you are what you appear to be from the distance.

Does that punch you in the gut like it did me? With the total realization that you are able to get by with determination and dedication to loving your family for a little while, but eventually you have nothing left to give?

We can go through the days like a shell of a person, focused on the little tasks at hand, feeling like we are barely hanging on to being a functional adult. We make sure our kids and spouse have what they need for dinner and for the next day. We do the dishes, the laundry, we sweep, we get the coffee pot ready, we clean up, we *insert the next mundane chore*. We make sure the kids are all tucked into bed and have every intention of NOW spending quality time with our spouse, only to crash because your mind, body, and soul are at the brink of exhaustion.

This <u>was</u> me. I NEVER gave undistracted, quality time to my children or my spouse. If I was sitting down, I was running through my head ALL of those things I just mentioned that just HAD to be done. But you know what I learned? I know people can tell you this all day and night, but you have to be able to understand it for yourself:

TIME WITH YOUR FAMILY IS SO MUCH MORE IMPORTANT THAN THE DISHES.

No wait, let me re-word that for all of you that are like me and know that, but are unable to practice that because you can't relax until all the chores are done. I knew that to be true. I know my family is more important than the dishes. But, what I couldn't realize until God helped me see it, is that my misguided sense of self-worth from making sure the chores were done, and my ridiculous notion that I couldn't relax if I knew that there were still dishes and laundry waiting on me, was from the enemy. Yes I said it. That sense of uneasiness and restlessness for ensuring chores is complete when you could be spending time with your family does NOT come from God. So, let's try this again.

WE ALLOW HAVING DIRTY DISHES, OR JUST THE DISTRACTION OF KNOWING THAT THEY ARE THERE, TO MEAN MORE TO US THAN QUALITY TIME WITH OUR FAMILY.

If something doesn't give you peace, it isn't what you should be doing.

Do you ever sit down to spend time with your Bible, a devotional, your family, only to jump back up because you suddenly remembered that you had to throw the clothes in the dryer first? So after you throw the clothes in the dryer, you notice that you need to sweep under the kitchen table, and then you see some toys that need to be put back into their place? The next thing you know it is 15 minutes past your kid's bedtime and you haven't spent one intentional minute with them the entire night? You haven't started your devotional and it is already 9pm. You haven't done one thing you have on your list of things you say are top priorities for you!

Hold tight with me here, I know you are thinking, "Yes I do that often, unfortunately, but what exactly does this have to do with a well? Where are you going with this?"

My husband often laughs at me because whenever I have a story to tell I have to tell him three stories to lead up to the main story I was wanting to share. My daughters have begun taking after me in that regard as well. It can be quite entertaining. Especially when I finally get to the time of the main story I forget my point and why I was trying to wrap it all up with a little bow.

So here is the point. The point of why you have read these first few pages, and why you want to read the rest of these chapters.

You have to put God first, take care of yourself next, and then you can have the quality time with your family that you wish now that you had. It is as simple as that statement.

But how do we get there? I want to share with you how I did, and I pray that it helps you in your journey to fill your well and keep it full, so that all of those people you allow to come into your heart, and into your home, are able to have water to draw from. I want to show you how you can fulfill that promise to those who are coming to you for what you appear to be. Mom, wife, friend, coach, what you want to be, need to be, and say to be.

Faith. Family. Fitness. Finances. That is my motto. When I became a health and fitness mentor, I created a Facebook like page, and after praying on it, those things came to mind and have been at the forefront of the way I live since. The key is to remember the order in which they are placed. We will look at some of these in the next few chapters to help you gain a better understanding of how I have filled my well, and how you can fill yours too.

CHAPTER 2

Faith

Faith HAS TO come first. This is non-negotiable. To have a life in which you are happy, healthy, living intentionally, and able to give to others because you have something to give, your faith in God has to be first.

Now, I need to get real for a few minutes here. First, let me say that I truly and with my whole being believe that when you hear something that someone says that you or others should be and need to be doing or working on, if it offends you, repulses you, and/or completely turns you off to the idea or even to the individual that is voicing it, it is because it is something that YOU need to work on. It is something that you probably are not ready to take ownership of, to admit even to yourself.

So, when I share thoughts and ideas in the coming paragraphs and chapters, know it is out of love and a true spiritual desire to help others grow and wanting to help. I want you to have lifelong changes, not just getting excited while reading the book but not having any actions that you are taking once you set it on the bookshelf when you are done. We can read and learn all day long, but it won't mean much if we never act on those things we learn.

I can say this because I know it is my truth. When someone says something and it feels offensive, it's because I already know in my heart it is something I am lacking in but not ready to work on it. Does it feel like I am building up to something? Are you ready to put this book down because I might offend you?

Good! It means that you have admitted in your deepest of thoughts, and heart, that you have things in your life that you need to work on. You are ready to hear those things, because you are ready to break free from what is holding you back and grow. Read this, set it down and ponder, come back and reread. Don't take these feelings you have for granted. Take notes and read them over and over. We are working through some things in this book. God did not put this message in my heart to entertain or be superficially motivating for a few days until you read the last page. We are in this for the long haul. We are getting ready to make some life changes. Soak this in until it reaches your soul and that piece of your heart that you know needs to be repaired.

So let us have faith with the Lord and trust that you will get more than just a good read out of this book, you will know what mountain you are meant to move. I pray in this moment that you are able to come closer to our mighty God through the words in this books and the actions that you take to fulfill what it is you are meant to do. I ask God to lift you and cover you in love, confidence, determination, and to have the desire to fill your well so that you may give to others and share what it is that you, and you alone, are meant to do.

CHAPTER 3

Fear

Let's get over this right here near the beginning. What is the thing that you fear? What dreams and desires do you have in your heart that negative thoughts in your head keep at a distance? What is that thing that you wanted to do ever since you can remember but it is just a dream? Do you think that maybe, just maybe, that is your calling? We don't grow and reach that level God has called us to reach in our comfort zones. Without the struggle, you don't have a story. You don't have lessons learned without pushing yourself into something uncomfortable.

What has fear and doubt kept you from your whole life? THAT is so very likely where God needs you to be. The doubt that stands in your way is the indication that the enemy needs to fight you to reaching that. It takes some practice to be able to be ok with being afraid, but you HAVE to push through it. Does it help to get over the fear if you know that the fear is the enemy trying to stop you from fulfilling your destiny, interrupting that life that God has for you? Because that is what fear is. God gives you peace, He will be there when you do those things that aren't easy for you. Can you imagine if you were too afraid to take that step to go in front of the church and announce that Jesus died on the cross for you and the Holy Spirit has filled you with the conviction to ask for forgiveness for your sins? I was pretty terrified in that specific moment, but I KNEW that what God needed from me and had for me was SO MUCH MORE than that ridiculous fear.

If you can't say for certain that you can push into a bit of fear throughout this book, I want you to stop reading for today, pray on it, ask God to help you with the difficulty you may face and come back when you can accept a bit of uncomfortableness. I can say for certainty, if you are reading this right now, you are meant to hear what I am about to share with you. But YOU need to know you are ready to hear it as well.

If you truly do feel like you have to address some issues with fear before continuing with this book, join us on my Facebook page Elizabeth D. Too Blessed to be Stressed. There we will embrace you and help you through the fear so that you can come back to this book with strength and willingness to grow that you can only receive from God himself.

CHAPTER 4

Filling the Well-Practically

To have a full well, we have to begin by addressing what it is that drains us.

One thing that was and can still be a huge issue for me is food. Food is meant to nourish our bodies and increase our energy, right? So, why would I say that it can drain me and empty MY well (and so many of yours)? Because of the stress, the shame, the time, and the mental energy that I would spend concerning myself with food. I would stress eat. I would eat out of boredom and sadness. I would eat as a reward for a goal reached, or eat as a celebration. I used to think about it and let it consume my thoughts to an unhealthy extreme. I knew what I was supposed to do. I knew that eating according to the my specific eating plan is what works best for my body. But why would I not stay consistent with it? Is it that bad habits take over? Maybe a little. Is it that I am not disciplined or strong enough? Absolutely not! It is so much more than that, I would binge eat, stress eat, and eat out of boredom because of some sort of **subconscious punishment to myself**. Are you punishing yourself with food? Pause here and pray over this if it hits home with you. I know that I needed a moment there too. Take your time, and remember, this is a process.

I could be happy, healthy, and have energy for weeks, for months sometimes, and then I let the enemy in, and believe that I don't deserve to feel well. I would doubt that I deserved happiness or consistency, and those negative thoughts would be physically manifested through eating badly, or in a way that I knew would not make me feel my best. I would sabotage myself out of a feeling of not being good enough to deserve what I had accomplished.

I believe that all of us self-sabotage in some way, until we can break free from it. So, how do you self-sabotage? For me it was food. Is it something that you know you are good at but don't do because it seems hard, there is not enough time in the day? Is it letting yourself feel stress at a job that you used to love, but now are so stressed you feel like you would do anything you could, to be able to leave?

Let me let you in on a little secret.

It is not the job that is causing you the stress. It is YOU allowing stress to consume you, to enter your heart and mind. It is self-sabotaging to let yourself feel stress when you used to let those same things when you first started working there, roll off your back like they were no big deal. You may not feel appreciated, you may feel like someone is treating you badly, you may feel as though you aren't meant to be there. But I want to remind you, God has a plan for you, and that plan is for you to be exactly where you are right now, in this very moment. The enemy is whispering in your ear and your heart that you are stressed, that this "thing" is not worth it. But more importantly, we to right now remember this: that God gives you peace.

Let me relate what needs to be said next to food, since that was **my** self-sabotaging behavior. I do not know statistics on this, but I can be fairly certain from experience in speaking with so many other women about nutrition and exercise, that most women my age, have some sort of issue, past or present, with food. So I know that you can relate to this, and I pray that this will resonate with all of you.

When we are hungry, we eat, right? When I am hungry, I get food. When I think I am hungry, I get food. We agree on this so far don't we? Just for a moment, let's pretend that we aren't hungry for food.

What else would we be hungry for?

We are hungry for love, for affection, for fulfillment, for mercy, for grace, for forgiveness, for redemption, for life, for the voice of God speaking to us. Yet, somehow we turn all of these needs and desires we are hungry for, into a reason to eat food. We won't be satisfied with food when we hunger for these things.

Of course I know that we need to eat to sustain ourselves, to live. I most certainly will not argue with that. But the boundary I am willing to push with you is that we do not always just eat to sustain us to live. When was the last time you ate because if you didn't you would perish? We are all first world dwellers who could stand to miss a meal if it so happened that we didn't have access to food for a day or two. But we don't, many of us cannot recall the last time we went an entire day without food. So, our hunger is not always, or even usually about food. Can you agree with me on that at least a little? Somehow we find it easier to believe that we need food to satisfy our hunger, rather than address what it is we are truly hungry for.

When we can feed ourselves the right way, with the right things, our well will be filled. Our well will be sustained, and it will thrive.

Are you ready to do this with me? It is time to get practical. When I wrote this, it was intended to be set up to have a daily thought, task, prayer, or action. I also know that when I was writing this book, that if you are anything like me, you have a great desire to continue to read, to finish what you started, to get ahead of the timeline, to check it off of your To-Do list. I am not saying you can't do that, but I am saying that I know how this works, it worked for me, so in that, I pray that you can trust the process and take it as you are supposed to day by day, week by week, or even month by month.

Let the time have an effect on you so that you can fully let everything in the process sink in. If you rush, you may very well be planting the seeds I am able to share with you, but they are not there long enough to let roots begin to grow.

The *roots* of what this book will give you, come from completing the actions each day as scheduled, in order. You will be intentional, and you will be sensitive to the fact that you need roots to maintain the information and allow it to stick around for years to come.

You can read through the entire book and then go back to week one and start with the practical application if you choose. I know that I don't necessarily expect you to wait six weeks to begin working out. Some of these things can be done together. But I want you to know is that this is a process and if you try to do everything at once, it will be so much harder to stick with it, or to actually be able to continuously and for long-term, fill your well. When you get to the week, shift your focus to what we are working on, while still implementing what you learned the week before. By giving yourself time to fix your focus, you will allow yourself to have success.

Time in between the chapters will grow your actions into something sustainable and rooted in truth and prayer.

Can you let that sink in today and begin your practical applications tomorrow? I would love for you to head over to my Facebook page and tell me that you are ready to fill your well!

WEEK 1

Shift Your Focus

Have you ever bought something you were totally in love with and knew it was great, it was special, maybe even unique, and then not long after you got it, you notice that everyone everywhere suddenly has one too? A vehicle is a perfect example.

I recently upgraded my white Ford Explorer with a newer year white Ford Explorer. The older one was not anything special, just a vehicle that got me from point A to point B, a vehicle with reliability. Because it was older and just a mode of transportation, I never gave it much thought, but in comparison, the newer one was GREAT! It was a bit of a different body style, it had more features, and more upgrades. Let's just say it was a step up and I was pleased with it.

Now as I drive to work every day, I see at least two on the way and four other white explorers in my work parking lot. Really! They are not new, they have always been there, I had just never focused on them. It was not important to me.

You will start noticing things that are similar to yours because you changed your focus. In this instance, I was focusing on my new to me vehicle, so I now started to see them everywhere. I was not focused on the old one because it did not matter to me, isn't interesting how that works?

Do you see where I am going with this? When you focus on what is important, you start to see more of it. You see it everywhere you turn. Focus. What are we focusing on?

Today and for the week, I want you to focus on God. When you begin to shift your focus to Him and are pleased with His amazingness, you will begin to see His work everywhere. Just like me and the white explorers. (Ok, so I am not putting a vehicle and God in the same realm of comparison, but if you are anything like me, the visualization of something relatable makes the Lord and His gracefulness and goodness something that I can almost comprehend.)

For the next 7 days, shift your focus on God. What things remind you of Him? What reminds you of His grace, goodness, forgiveness, compassion, or beauty?

We will write down 5 things that remind You of Him. We are going to look at them over and over again this week. Don't just read them, feel the emotions that are attached with them. An example for me would be the feeling of peace I get when I look at the sky. When I look up and see it, I instantaneously feel closer to God. So every time I go outside, I stop for a few moments and take a deep breath, and appreciate that beauty.

Another example would be my kids. When I get frustrated with never having a moment to myself, (moms you understand this, right? I mean, we rarely even pee alone) I take a deep breath and thank God for giving me these beautiful girls to raise. I do not ever want to know what silence feels like because I don't have them anymore.

So let's think about those five things that God has blessed YOU with to remember Him. What are they?

1. _____

2. _____

3. _____

4. _____

5. _____

At the end of each day, after an entire week of you working on remembering these things that keep you close to God, share not only what they are with someone, but also share how your week went when you shifted your focus. It can be your spouse, a parent, a close friend, a book club where you are all working through this together, just be sure to share it. If you don't have anyone, come on over to my Facebook page and share it with me. I would love to hear what keeps you close to Him and help you continue to focus on those things.

This exercise is something that you will need more than a week to perfect. To fully shift your focus, it will need to be second nature, a habit. But, once you have it down, it will change your life. Fall asleep tonight and every night thanking Him for these five things that you wrote down.

Tomorrow is a new day with a new chapter, not only in this book, but in you living intentionally and having a well full enough to pass what you have on to others, and that is the goal we have right now isn't it?

WEEK 2

Get Rid of the Weight

Before we metaphorically fill up our well, we need to let go of what is weighing us down. To go back and use my visualization of you being the well, picture this: Even if the well is full of water, no one will be able to lift the bucket to get the water if something is weighing that bucket down. So we need to get rid of what is weighing us down.

This is not a simple thing. If it was, none of us would have this problem. This isn't something that will be done in one week, but it is something that you need to start today. Just like week one, this will take some practice. You will need to come back to this whenever you have certain feelings, but practice and consistency will make it easier.

Think about this, although I am sure you may have this thought quite often. *What are you not?* I am not asking who you think you are, who others think you are, I want you to say what you think you are not. We have all this negative self-talk and labels that we give ourselves, those things that we would be afraid to say out loud because in all reality, we know that there is a very slim chance that anyone else thinks that we are not good enough.

Why do we talk to ourselves so terribly, label ourselves, and call ourselves names? We have the thoughts like this, the thoughts of "I am not a good mom, I am probably ruining my kids." "I am not pretty, I am not in shape, or I am not a good cook." These are the thoughts I am talking about here, and we need to get rid of these thoughts replace them with the thoughts that *others* think when they look at you.

Write down the negative things that you consistently think about yourself. What are a few things you are not? Be specific and start each with "I am not…"

1. _____
   _____

2. _____
   _____

3. _____
   _____

4. _____
   _____

5. _____
   _____

Now, ask your spouse and each child (or best friend, mom, etc.) to give you five things to finish this sentence. Try to get more than one person to answer this for you, the more responses you get from different people, the faster you will be able to see yourself for who others see you as, as you really are.

"Your name" (i.e. mom) is....

1. _____
   _____
2. _____
   _____
3. _____
   _____
4. _____
   _____
5. _____
   _____

It is that simple of a statement. I would be willing to bet that no one you asked has the same thing on their list about you that you put about yourself.

You have such a narrow set of blinders on about yourself that you cannot see the truth.

Why define who you are by a handful of negative things when the good things far outweigh those things you put on the first list?

What we need to do for the next few days is to spend some time reflecting on what others answered when you asked them what you are.

This is such a difficult thing to do, so I want to share with you that I know from my own personal experience that this is essential to change, and I know it is hard, but more importantly, I know it is worth it.

Somedays we will need to look at the list that others said about us and remind ourselves that the negative self-talk in our head is false. It will never completely go away, but we can equip ourselves to fight it and throw it out as nonsense as soon as it enters our mind. The big terrible things I used to have in my head are long gone from following these steps.

However, there are occasionally some smaller, quieter thoughts that creep in, like no one would want to read that book, why write it, or you're not good enough. You know why I am able to throw those out? Because I know I got rid of the big stuff, and I know how far I have come, and how I won't let some little thought in my head derail me from the purpose I know God has for me.

Not everyone will like my book. But I can assure you, if it helps one person to change their life like it has changed mine, I did what He needed me to do. Your heart has to be ready to address these problems and work towards living a life you don't want to be in. We do this by putting one foot in front of the other and don't stop. We keep moving. It takes the same amount of energy to stay the same as it does to change.

WEEK 3

No More Comfort Zone

Let's think about what it feels like in our comfort zone. It is comforting and comfortable because there is no unknown. Even if where you are is terrible, it can still be comforting knowing what the outcome is and not wondering or being nervous or afraid of what is to come. But, let me tell you this, and I know you hear it often, but really listen this time. YOU CANNOT GROW STAYING IN YOUR COMFORT ZONE.

Think about that comfort zone, and then we are going to throw it out the window. In today's society of instant gratification and social media obsession, we have come to a point where we expect a finished product. We want to see people at their best and then we feel inferior because we aren't living up to what we believe is their normal. Those people who always look incredible in their selfies probably took 65 pictures to get that one. There are filters applied to pictures, people only taking pictures from certain angles and in certain light. The people that are always taking selfies know how and at what angle they look best.

Our world has come to actually glorify the finished product. We need to remember that God glorifies us as being a work in progress. We all want to see people who have lost a ton of weight, look amazing in pictures, seemingly have it all put together, baking cupcakes for their kids classes while dressed in the latest fashion, all while having an immaculate house, and perfect children. The truth is, no one has that life. No one. What we portray on social media is what we choose to show others. Who wants to show themselves as a work in progress? Not many. But I will tell you, if you can remember that God is glorifying our work in progress, you will think differently about it. Stop glorifying the finished product and start telling yourself that God is glorifying us as the work in progress.

Listen to me for a minute, and I want to tell you that I am saying this out of personal experience. Everything in this book is something that I needed to hear myself before I found the key to having a full well.

If I stayed in my comfort zone, I wouldn't have helped you with knowing that there is a way out of stress eating, over eating, under eating, if I wouldn't have shared my experiences with you and stayed in my comfort zone of pretending none of those things ever had happened to me, I couldn't have helped anyone. If I hadn't shared that I too have feelings of shame, of not being good enough, about hiding things in the past, I wouldn't have helped YOU know that sharing is the way out of that craziness. We have to share our hurt and our story, to grow. You don't have to put it all in a book like I am, but you can share it with someone individually.

A personal example is this: when I shared a video on Facebook recently about how the eating plan I use helped me so much with stress eating, I got ONE comment on the video. ONE! But let me let you in on this behind the surface of only having on like on a post, what I also got, was 15 private messages that were just between that one individual and I, sharing that the video helped them and they have that problem too! We have to get out of our comfort zone and <u>know</u> we are not alone. If I went by the fact that no one commented publically on that post, I would have deleted it a half hour later and not helped any of those ladies that sent me messages. We need to reach out past where we want to stay to be comfortable to get out of where we are! If we aren't stretching, there is NO WAY we can move.

Admitting it is just the beginning. Of those fifteen ladies that told me that they were ready to change and wanted more info on how to do it, only a couple actually went through with investing in themselves and getting out of that day to day mundane sameness. You have to be ready too. I promise you, that initial step is the hardest. I share things that are uncomfortable for me ALL THE TIME. Why? Because if I can help one person, me feeling uncomfortable is worth it.

So, how do we do this…? It will be tough to write it down, but you need to! When I first was given this idea for the book, it couldn't come out fast enough, and I tried to talk-text it into a notes app on my phone, and I could not say some of those things in my introduction out loud. Why? Because I never had. I have typed them, but never said them out loud. See, we are all still a work in progress, and I am working on speaking my truth even though sharing it on paper is becoming easier.

What one thing do you want to forget about most, what thing are you ashamed of, or hope no one ever finds out? I am not going to make a space for you to write it down in the book, but you need to write it down somewhere. What is it?

You know that thing you are having a hard time writing down or mad at me for making you think about? THAT is what God needs you to share to grow. Like I said, it doesn't have to be a public declaration on all social media outlets. Share it with a friend, a spouse, a stranger, message me and share it. But you have to share it!

The reason that this one thing is put into an entire chapter is that it is supposed to last you an entire week, it is because I know that it is a simple thing to do, but it is not easy, it is HARD! It isn't something to be taken lightly, and it isn't something that you have on your heart right now. Maybe it is something that you have pushed so deep down into forgetting that you cannot even recall it right now.

God is gracious, and forgiving, and loving, and He gave His only son for us to mess up. He let us get ourselves into something so that we know it is Him who gets us out, and part of that process is showing progress. It isn't about forgetting, it is about moving forward and being ok with being uncomfortable, so that maybe, we can help one or more other people who are going through something similar.

This week is dedicated to working on this, don't put this book down and stop reading because you don't like this part. This is your time to change, your time to grow, and your time to help someone else.

Once you can do this, we can move onto filling our well. This was the hard part! Filling us up with the good stuff now that we have dropped the weight and shame of the bad stuff, is the best part!

WEEK 4

Personal Development

We are starting to figure out how to fill our well now. We have shifted our focus and thrown out comfort zones. We have figured out what was weighing us down and now we are free and clear to fill up! It you still feel weighed down, go back to the previous weeks and work on them again. For some it may take twice as long to get rid of that "weight" than it may for others. We aren't rushing, we are working through this and we need to do it right for it to be lasting.

So, what is personal development? It is reading, watching, and listening to things that keep your spirits up, get you motivated and inspired. This is to ensure you keep growing and working on yourself. I read books, a lot of them, but I also know that some people aren't like me, and could live in a library or a Barnes & Noble. If you aren't one of those people who love books, go to YouTube, get audio books to listen to in the car, or put on a podcast while you are folding laundry or doing the dishes.

If you struggle with something specifically, find a podcast or book that addresses that issue. You are reading this because you are sick and tired of being sick and tired. You want to feel alive again, have energy and live intentionally, right? I love that you are here with me in this, working through being better, but you can't stop here. This small step of continued personal development, truly does make the biggest impact in your life.

I heard a statistic the other day, that said most Americans read on average, one book a year and most millionaires in America read an average of 60 books a year. I cannot tell you if that is completely accurate, but it says something about being successful, don't you think? To me it shows that we always have to be willing to learn and know we can always continue to grow.

Come on over to my Facebook page, or email me if you need a recommendation for audio, video, or books to help you with a specific situation. In my business, we are always sharing new personal development we find.

Start with ten minutes a day. You will begin to crave it because it is filling your well. Filling a need in your life you may or may not have even realized was there. You could follow someone on Facebook that inspires you, and motivates you to be better.

This is not a difficult thing to do, you just have to know that it is something you need, and be willing and excited to make it a priority.

In my work, the job requires you to have ten minutes minimum a day of personal development. I hear ALL THE TIME that people skip this because they don't think they need it. But what people always seem to find is that it is the single thing that they needed the most. That when they actually did it, their business began to grow because they were growing too. They were sharing what they were inspired by, and it inspired others.

Let me share a personal example of how personal development has helped me. I read a book called Unashamed by Christine Caine earlier this year. I had, for many reasons, completely blocked out my teenage years. I joined the Army after high school, moved out of the state, not kept in touch with anyone from those years in my life, and when I would visit my parents, I would hope that I didn't run into anyone there. I was out one day and this book jumped out at me amongst a sea of books and it was on clearance at this particular store, I looked at it and set it back down. I decided not to get it. I went up to the register to pay for what I had and as the gentleman was ringing everything up, he held up that same book and asked if that was mine too. Someone had left it on the counter and it was beside all of my stuff, so he was not sure if I wanted it. I was smart enough to recognize a sign when I saw one, so I told him to add it to my bag.

I have read that book more than once and it is kept in a small stack of books I have on my dresser that have changed my life. It made me realize that I was ashamed of that time because of me, not because of all of these people I somehow had decided I needed to hide from. They didn't do anything, they just reminded me of a time I didn't want to remember.

So after that book, I reached out to as many high school friends as I could think of. Some didn't respond to me, but that is ok! The ones that did had no idea where I had disappeared to and were surprised to hear from me. I was able to catch up and reconnect with people I pushed away for no reason other than my shame.

Some of those people I have been able to reconnect with have reached out to me and shared how much I have inspired them by sharing my story and struggles. I made an everlasting impact on them because I was brave enough to get out of my comfort zone and reach out.

I highly recommend that book if you ever struggle with shame. In letting go of that shame and fear from that era of my life, I have regained some amazing friendships, that without personal development, I would have never had. My shame seemed so much smaller than what Christine shared of her story in her book and it gave me the courage to get over myself. That was worth everything.

WEEK 5

Get What You Give

You may or may not know this, but it is possible to get energy, to get happiness, to fill your well, by giving what it is you need. Yes, expending energy, being happy, and filling another's well, will give you that in which you are giving. The important thing to know about this though, is that not everything you give to can give you something in return.

We spend too much time and energy giving to things that can't help to fill our well. Things that drain us of energy, things we feel are not anything but stress.

I am in no way saying you have to stop giving energy to certain things, not at all. Some things we just need to change our perspective on the situation, and some things we need to do more of so that we can have the energy and happiness to give to other things also.

Where and what gives us energy when we give energy? Here is an example. Most nights, homework time is stressful in my house, and something I was not a fan of doing. I actually liked the fact that my kids after school program had them do homework and had checked it over before I picked them up, which meant we rarely ever discussed homework.

Well, they kind of have gotten away from that for a time, so I had been trying to fit it in while multitasking on other things. It was tiring and frustrating. One day not long ago, I sat with my oldest, and didn't have the T.V. on, didn't have my phone, just sat with her, and intentionally did her homework and talked everything through and made sure I was focusing only on her and helping her to be better, even though I didn't want to, because I knew it would be a draining experience. Well, can you imagine that it was an absolutely incredible experience? It really was. I felt a renewed sense of energy after that homework, and so did she. We were able to give to each other during the exchange. It happens with my younger daughter as well. When I sit down with them with no other thought than to help with their homework and give them love, focus, attention, and assistance, I feel all of that in return!

When your kids or spouse come up to you and have a question, comment, concern, and you are doing something else, make eye contact, and don't say "hang on". See how much it changes how you feel, how refreshed and happy you feel after those undistracted moments. You will begin to crave them, because it is what your soul needs.

We have become so ok with thinking we have to multitask every second of every day that how could we not be drained? We do not need to multitask when it causes you to be distracted on what matters most. Your family, those you love, that is what matters. So stop doing things that don't matter while the things that do matter are standing right in front of you!

This may be a work in progress for you for a long time. It is for me, I still struggle with it, but I also have had years and years of thinking that multitasking was essential to survival, so it takes time to break those thought patterns.

(In editing this book, I had to stop here, for quite some time, and reflect on the fact that I had once again gotten away from this. I too often, even recently hear my name called ten times because I am distracted with something else. I needed to fix my focus again on this, and God led me to it again this day He reminded me to edit. Remember, we are all ALWAYS a work in progress, and if we can honor that truth, we are so much further ahead than most others.)

Here is a small task I can have you do right now. Do you have Facebook or Instagram? Good. I can safely assume that none of you are saying no to that question. I want you to find an inspirational saying, picture, or meme that means something to you and post it on your page. Go on, I'll wait.

Did you do it? Good. Now, tomorrow I want you to look at that post and see if anyone liked or commented on it. If you have more than five friends on those platforms, I can almost guarantee that someone liked it. You made a difference in that person's day. This will be huge if you don't normally post such things. You have to feel good knowing that you inspired someone, right? If you can continue this in small ways like that to inspire others or make someone else smile, be polite to them, or even just to say hello, you will have a full well. You will get so much more than you put out.

When you help to fill someone else's well, you are filling yours also. Next time you see someone online having a tough day, give them hope, tell them you see how hard they are working and how much they inspire you. You will be filling both their well and yours.

WEEK 6

Exercise

No, you cannot skip this chapter or working out. You can't. This is another one of those things that takes energy to get energy. Trust me on this.

If you don't work out already, start small. Begin taking more steps each day, jumping on the trampoline with your kids for three minutes. (I exercise daily and I have to say, I cannot last more than a couple minutes on a trampoline; that is <u>for sure</u> a workout.)

It has to be something that you enjoy. You won't stick with exercise if you feel like it is a job or a chore. I have learned that small changes are how I am able to be consistent with exercise. If I go from nothing to trying to work out an hour a day, I probably won't make it more than a week before I quit. I have a Fitbit and have found out first hand that if I walk in place for an hour while my husband and I are watching our favorite show, I will get in a couple thousand extra steps! I am expending a bit more energy than I would be sitting on the couch, but your body responds in an amazing way when you are consistent with it. You will sleep better and feel more rested, you will have MORE energy from using some.

If you have a desk job, get up every hour and walk down the hall. These small changes over time will add up to major changes and will fill your well. After a while you will have the energy to go out and play with your kids instead of watching them play. You will not only be exercising, but spending intentional quality time with them. You will give them memories. That is one thing that hit me hard when I began to focus on filling my well. Thinking about the memories that I was giving my kids. Every single time we went outside I would watch them play and every single time they would ask me to join them and I was always exhausted and said no. Having a full well and being able to join them now is one of the most precious gifts I have been able to give to myself and to them.

Part of my business is assisting people with health and fitness, finding what works for them. So I know that this is a process that is ongoing and you need support and accountability.

Sometimes you may get resistance from others because they see that you are working on yourself. Don't let that get you off track. It should motivate you more to stay with what it is you are doing. People are watching you, and when you show up every day with consistency and positivity, it won't be long before they want to know your secret. Ask them if they want to take a quick walk with you at lunch or after work. You will not only be exercising, but having a conversation that could very possibly be rewarding for the both of you.

Exercise is something that cannot be broadened enough for me to give you a "how-to" here. No one approach to exercise fits everyone, it is *for* you, and something you are going to be putting the effort into, which means that there is not a "do these ten steps and you'll feel better" task list. If you feel you are not equipped with the tools to make the determination to what you will be consistent with, reach out to me. That is what I love to do!

AFTER THE SIX WEEKS

As I briefly mentioned in the previous chapter, I have come to know from personal experience, that to be successful in anything, I need to make small changes that compound over time to "stick" and become lifelong changes. There have been way too many Mondays or New Year's resolutions in which I have a list of changes I need to make in my life and I am determined to master all of them starting tomorrow. I would check them off every day that I accomplish them, and not long after I start, I would miss a couple, which caused me to miss some more, and too soon after I had started, I had completely given up on ALL the changes I needed and wanted to make within my life. All because I was missing a couple checkmarks! I gave up on all of those things I knew were moving me in the direction I felt led. Have you ever done this too?

Maybe you aren't much like me in the way of making to do lists (and even sometimes adding something you just did to it so that you can cross it off), but I can guess if you have picked up this book and made it this far, you aren't always succeeding when you try to make a change. What I want to share here is that we cannot expect to one day wake up and make everything the way we picture it to be. We will only be setting ourselves up for failure with that expectation.

Once we have done this a few times and failed, we stop trying, we begin to accept the way we are and the life we are living as though it's impossible to change and it just "is what it is". THAT'S SO FAR

FROM THE TRUTH! That place is exactly where the enemy wants us, because if we are unhappy with our life, but have no desire to change it because we haven't been successful with it in the past, he wins. The enemy has kept you from the extraordinary life that God has for you.

So how do we stop letting the enemy win? We start small, slow, and build up the consistency and habits, and once we have a strong foundation, even if we falter on one thing, we don't and won't give up on everything! A small and slow pace is specific to the individual person and their specific circumstances.

Let me give you an example: When I wanted to get into shape and realized that I need to have the strong foundation that was built with blocks and not just trying to have the entirety of everything at once, I made the list of everything that I wanted to get right. This included working out daily, getting enough water, eating according to my plan, getting a set amount of sleep, drinking my shake, etc. I saw that list, and I picked two things, working out daily, and drinking my shake. Those would be a non-negotiable for me for the next 30 days. The other things were good to do too, but I didn't make them a task on my to-do list. So for 30 days I checked off those two things on my list and built a foundation. Day 31 I added getting enough water and working on my sleep. Now, I already had the foundation of the first month, so when I don't get enough sleep or drink enough water, the furthest I fall back is to those two things I just added. I don't stop working out and drinking my shake, because those are already habits and my foundation to being healthier.

What I am getting at by sharing this example with you is that it took me 30 days of doing two things consistently to make that foundation. You may know yourself enough to know that you only have to do a week, or maybe you need longer. You have to find what works for you. 30 days has been the golden ticket for me and building my pattern of good behaviors. The important thing is to know that you can't read this book and try to implement them all at once. You have to build one on the other and have that foundation. You may need to change the week into a month. That is ok. That is actually wonderful in my opinion, because <u>you know</u> you need more time to make it a habit.

Once you feel as though it has become a strong foundation into who you are, add another chapter. Like I said, I put "weeks" on the chapter titles, but I will be the first to admit to you that I spent a month or more on some of these action steps before I was prepared to move on to the next. The information I shared about getting out of your comfort zone, I still have to work on that often. There is no way that could have been my first chapter, my foundation.

I may have mentioned this to you earlier, but I am a visual person. I can see or hear potentially life changing information in a hundred ways from a hundred different people and perspectives and it may not mean anything to me. Then, that one person can share that same thought with a visualization I can comprehend, and I GET IT. It then make sense. It clicks.

I say this because I want to give you a visualization when I talk about a foundation if it isn't making sense to you, or if it isn't yet a life altering thought, and if you still plan to try and do all of this at once. Are you still with me here?

Roots. As in tree and plant roots. I mentioned them earlier. How do they work? I am not a tree expert by any means, but I do know that it takes time, and the longer amount of time that the roots are given to grow and flourish, the bigger, stronger, and harder they are to destroy. If something is newly planted, you can rip it out of the ground easily. If it has been given time and allowed to grow and stretch, the roots become the foundation for the tree and allow it to become solid, not shaky, or something that will be knocked over or die in a strong wind.

Now, can you take the thought and visualize a tree that is a hundred years old and picture the roots stretching far away from that tree and really think about how big and strong they are. They were allowed to grow and prosper. Now take that same visualization and put it into YOU. Things that you are doing to be the best version of you. Each day you are making your roots deeper and stronger, so that a strong wind won't derail you.

The moment God gave me this book, I knew that He is what makes my roots stronger, He makes them sustain heavy winds and storms. We all know that being a Christian doesn't mean that we won't face storms, it means that we know we have strong roots that will allow us to get through it with the assurance that He is with us.

I want these practical things within this book to be part of your root system, but it all must start with God. Each time you implement a change, first get to a quiet space and ask Him to show you the way to make the changes long lasting. Ask Him to be with you when things get tough and you want to back down.

You are so close to making the life that He wants for you, you just have to remember in tough times that we are strong because of Him, and that we have roots that will keep us upright in the truth that we are meant to thrive and not be afraid of our past or what people will think of us.

You've made it this far into the book, so as we wrap up I would like you to put down some thoughts that are running through your mind right now on the following questions:

How do you feel about the strength of your faith? Is it very strong, weak, or non-existent? What could you do to make it stronger? Name three things that you could implement right now that would help build that strength. Remember, you don't live in your comfort zone anymore. It isn't just about those things you are used to doing, think big and list them below.

_____

_____

_____

_____

_____

_____

_____

_____

_____

_____

_____

_____

_____

_____

_____

The next question, now that we have addressed our most important well filling activity, which is getting closer to God and asking Him to guide us in filling our well and making us a better person, is about fear.

I know we already addressed it. We are doing it again. Why? Because most of you skipped over it the first time, or maybe did the exercise, but only got to some surface fears that you knew would be easier to address. So let's look at it again.

What irrational fears do you have that you know that still need to be addressed? The reason that I say irrational is because I can tell you from my personal experiences, as well as helping others get past fear, we agree that most are irrational. Those fears are the ones that you think are things that come easy to others, but not for you. Those things that you say you are afraid to do but you know that other people are comfortable with them.

A fear of mine has always been public speaking. You know, a fear I have had as long as I can remember, a crippling fear that led me to fail a high school class <u>twice,</u> because of my refusal to get up in front of the class and present a book report. The fear that led me to plead with God to find me another job when I was offered an instructor position that paid really well. I told myself that speaking in front of groups of people was for other people who are comfortable with it, not for me, that it was not what *I* was meant to do.

How do I know this was irrational? Because I hear public speakers all the time say the similar things. The most inspiring and motivating people I hear talk, say that they too are afraid or were afraid of public speaking.

Honestly, for the longest time, I just thought that they were lying and that I was just different. Think about this for a few moments. The things like this that you are fearful of are holding you back from your greatness. What if you thought about it like I do? Try thinking about this…The enemy is putting those fears in you because he knows that the Lord needs you to use that specific thing to fulfill your Godly purpose! That fear is the enemy fighting Gods purpose for you, he is making sure you fear exactly what God is calling you to do so that you won't fulfill that amazing life of purpose you are meant to. Read that again. Read it again. It was a total life changing moment for me when I realized this, when I realized that the enemy isn't fighting me, he is fighting my God, my Savior, the One who blesses me beyond anything I deserve.

Sometimes we aren't strong enough to protect ourselves, but we surely will protect others, right? So maybe you need to think about it like I did. I may not be strong enough to fight for myself at this very moment, not yet. But I surely am strong enough to protect and fight for my God. The enemy WILL NOT use ME to hurt my God!

Write that fear or fears here:

_____
_____
_____
_____
_____
_____
_____
_____
_____
_____

Ok. Now do this with me. Pray.

Lord, help me to stay in Your truth and Your word. Give me the strength to address these fears and the knowledge to know that they are irrational and come from the enemy. Help me to throw these fears out the window. God I am ready! I am ready to see the miracles that you can do *through* me. Your love, compassion, forgiveness, and strength is so much more than I deserve and I desire deeply to walk by my faith in You and not by my sight of worldly things. Allow me to see the right people and the right circumstances that will help me to grow closer to You. In Jesus name, AMEN!

Do you have a prayer you want to add to this after reading this? Add it here. Read some of God's word, ask Him to show you what you need to see in it; meditate on it for as long as you need and finish the prayer.

_____
_____
_____
_____
_____
_____
_____

Now, we are at the end. Not the end of what you need to do to fill your well, and not the end of putting these things into practice. But the end of this practical guide to a purposeful life.

This is probably the most action filled short book you will ever read and explore, and some people may want more pages. Let me ask you this if you are disappointed in the length of this book if I could. Have you gone through it and done the exercises? Have you prayed on these things, gone back and reread and let thinks sink in? I will have to say that you may need to go back and pray God shows you what you need to see in this book. Because I know it is short, but I also know that it is EXACTLY what helped me live a meaningful and intentional life. It is also EXACTLY what God has shown me to share with you. I prayed over each word in this book and asked the Lord to allow it to have meaning to you in a way only He can do.

Are you ready? Ready to begin implementing these things? Let's do this. Together, and with God first.

EXTRA CREDIT

As I look at what helps me on an ongoing basis, I am including some additional thoughts and actions you can take each day to ensure you are staying the course of filling the well.

God wants us to meditate on HIS word. For me, that took a long time. I would read all about the Bible, and I would study devotionals daily, I even started the Bible in a Year program. All of those are absolutely great, and something we should all strive to do, but I never got into the actual words that were written and meditated on them. So the following pages are specific verses that spoke to me. Read one and meditate on it. Write down any thoughts you may have on it. Come back and do it again if you need to.

Hebrews 4:12 says that "The word of God is alive and active…" When I recently had someone share this with me, I meditated on it, really focused on what God was trying to show me. It led to some incredible thoughts and ideas on how I can share His word with others and do things I enjoy and glorify Him at the same time.

This is an extra credit challenge. Not necessary as the rest of the practical exercises I have shared, but wonderful and fulfilling none the less.

Do you accept the challenge? Take one page and meditate on the verse. Jot down below what you heard or felt. (All verses are from the NLT.) This is something you should do when you feel led to do it.

It is an ongoing practice, and one that you can even do for yourself when you see a verse that jumps out at you. This practice is meant to be continual and long lasting. We don't need to answer them all in one day. You can even look at one for days and continue to write down what it is He is showing you with it.

Don't worry about it being complete thoughts, or neat, just write down what you feel and hear. You can sort through it all later. Just make sure you write it down as it comes.

Joshua 1:8

Study this Book of instruction continually. Meditate on it day and night so you will be sure to obey everything written in it. Only then will you prosper and succeed in all you do.

NOTES:

Philippians 2:13

For God is working in you, giving you the desire and the power to do what pleases Him.

NOTES:

Galatians 6:9

So let's not get tired of doing what is good. At just the right time we will reap a harvest of blessing if we don't give up.

NOTES:

2 Timothy 1:7

For God has not given us a spirit of fear and timidity, but of power, love, and self-discipline.

NOTES:

Luke 8:15

And the seeds that fell on the good soil represent honest, good-hearted people who hear God's word, cling to it, and patiently produce a huge harvest.

NOTES:

Psalms 139:23-24

Search me, O God, and know my heart; test me and know my anxious thoughts. Point out anything in me that offends you, and lead me along the path of everlasting life.

NOTES:

Proverbs 16:3

Commit your actions to the Lord, and your plans will succeed.

NOTES:

Galatians 1:10

Obviously, I'm not trying to win the approval of people, but of God. If pleasing people were my goal, I would not be Christ's servant.

NOTES:

ABOUT THE AUTHOR

Elizabeth Durden was born and raised in a small town in Maine. When she was 18 years old and more lost than she had ever been, she got out the only way she could see how, by joining the Army. For the next six years, she spent time in Hawaii, Texas, Alabama, and Iraq. It was after OIF I that she decided that she couldn't go through another deployment. She left the Army and got married shortly after to a service member. It was then she moved to Indiana and then Virginia and had two beautiful children. While living in Virginia she went through a devastating divorce which caused her to feel the need to leave her job and move back to Maine.

She was then led to an amazing man who is now her husband of three years. They live in a small town in rural Virginia, have found the Lord, raise chickens, and live a laid back rural life.

She is an online health and fitness mentor who has a purpose driven passion for helping others lead the life they are meant to lead. The life God has in store for them.

This book was a scary thing for her to do, but she knows when God calls, you answer.

If you found this book useful, share it, and let her know! Email her with notes, thoughts, or results that you have from implementing these changes, even things you would like to see from her next book.

She can be reached at:

CoachElizabethDurden@gmail.com with the Subject: Filling the Well

You can also follow her journey at Elizabeth D.- Too Blessed to be Stressed Facebook page.

Made in the USA
Las Vegas, NV
15 March 2023

69145511R00046